Besties

DELUXE
DECDER

Hidden MESSAGES
Unsolved MYSTERIES
Secret DECODER

FINE print
PUBLISHING

BESTIES
DELUXE
DECODER

CREATED BY
MICKEY
& CHERYL
GILL

FINE print
PUBLISHING

Fine Print Publishing Company
P.O. Box 916401
Longwood, Florida 32791-6401

Created in the USA & Printed in China
This book is printed on acid-free paper.

ISBN 978-1-892951-90-8

2 3 5 7 9 10 8 6 4 1

fprint.net

CLASSIFIED

AGENT

Mariah.

Your Name

BEAUTIFUL BUTTERFLIES

SPYING ON NEIGHBORHOODS.

MYSTERIOUS DOCUMENTS

BEING DROPPED AT YOUR DOOR.

A FAMOUS HEIRESS LEADING A

DOUBLE LIFE.

EACH CASE,
FROM SPYING EYES
TO MISSING AGENTS,
STARTS WITH A CODE.

AND WITH YOUR
ANYTHING-BUT-SECRET
INTELLIGENCE AND A
DELUXE DECODER RING,
YOU'LL CRACK EVERY
SINGLE ONE OF THEM.

HOW TO USE YOUR
DELUXE DECODER RING

DECIDE ON THE MESSAGE YOU WANT TO SEND.

 TRY THE MESSAGE **WATCH OUT FOR TRAPS**

Look for the first letter of your message — **W** — in the ring's inner circle.

W is not there. So look for it in the outer circle. Spin the ring's outer circle until you see the letter **W** appear in the small window.

The letter that lines up directly below the letter in the window is your first encoded letter.

Look for the second letter of your message — **A** — in the ring's inner circle first. Now spin the ring's outer circle until the window lines up directly above the letter.

The letter that appears in the window is your second encoded letter.

Continue until you have completely encoded your original message.

Your coded message should read —
JNGPU BHG SBE GENCF

Inner circle
Outer circle
Window

W = J

A = N

FOLLOW THE SAME STEPS TO DECODE A MESSAGE.

CODES VS. CIPHERS

CRACK THE CODE SOUNDS MORE AWESOME THAN CRACK THE CIPHER!

SO, YOU'LL SEE THE WORD **CODE** USED MORE IN YOUR CASES. BUT REMEMBER, MOST **CODES** ARE REALLY **CIPHERS**.

HERE'S THE DIFFERENCE.

CODES REPLACE AN ENTIRE WORD WITH A SET OF LETTERS, NUMBERS, OR SYMBOLS THAT ARE MADE-UP.

SO THE WORD LEMON COULD BE #28.

CIPHERS REPLACE EACH LETTER IN A WORD WITH ANOTHER NUMBER, LETTER, OR SYMBOL.

SO THE WORD LEMON COULD BE YRZBA.

encode – convert into a coded form

encipher – convert a message or piece of text into cipher

decode – convert a code into language that can be understood

decipher – translate from secret or mysterious writing into normal language

encrypt – convert information or data into a cipher or code

decrypt – make a coded or unclear message understandable

YOU ARE AN OFFICIAL UNDERCOVER AGENT.

ANSWER SOME TOP SECRET QUESTIONS SO HEADQUARTERS CAN ASSIGN YOU A FIELD AGENT POSITION.

START HERE

FIRST, CIRCLE THE ANSWERS THAT SOUND MOST LIKE YOU.

FAVORITE KIND OF SATURDAY?

1. Doing as many different, awesome things as possible.
2. Sleeping in and taking it easy for the rest of the day.
3. Doing something totally crazy with my friends.

HOW WOULD YOUR TEACHER(S) DESCRIBE YOU?

1. Gets along with teachers and lots of different kinds of kids.
2. Cool going solo or spending time with a few friends.
3. Very friendly but a little mischievous.

THERE'S A CITYWIDE VOLUNTEER CLEANUP DAY. YOU:

1. sign up on your own.
2. go because your parents make you.
3. volunteer with a group of friends but goof off too much.

HOW DARING ARE YOU?

1. Sort of but usually cautious.
2. Not. I'd rather relax.
3. Very! It's exciting!

BEST THING ABOUT A FAIR OR THEME PARK?

1. Time with friends
2. Food
3. Roller coasters!

YOUR TEACHER LEAVES THE CLASSROOM FOR A FEW MINUTES. YOU:

1. talk to the kids sitting next to you.

2. kick back and chill at your desk.

3. walk around the room and visit with all your friends.

DO YOU LIKE LEARNING OTHER LANGUAGES?

1. Yes, it's fun.

2. It's OK.

3. Not really.

WOULD YOU LIKE TO LIVE IN ANOTHER COUNTRY?

1. I'm ready!

2. It might be OK.

3. No.

WHAT KIND OF JOB SOUNDS AMAZING?

1. Corporate president

2. Resort hotel employee

3. Outdoor sports & activities instructor

WHO ARE YOU IN YOUR GROUP OF FRIENDS?

1. The leader

2. The cool one

3. The fun one

KEEP GOING

NEXT, ADD UP ALL THE NUMBERS YOU CIRCLED. IF YOUR TOTAL IS:

10-16, YOUR CODE IS — QBHOYR

17-23, YOUR CODE IS — FYRRCRE

24-30, YOUR CODE IS — CEBIBXRE

WRITE YOUR CODE HERE.

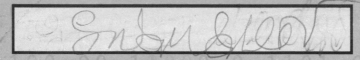

USE YOUR DELUXE DECODER RING TO DECIPHER YOUR CODE AND ENTER IT BELOW.

DELUXE
DECODER
RING

LOOK FOR YOUR DECIPHERED WORD IN THE LIST OF FIELD ASSIGNMENT POSITION DESCRIPTIONS.

AFTER YOU COMPLETE THE CASES INSIDE, HQ WILL INSTALL YOU AS A:

DOUBLE AGENT/OPERATIVE

Infiltrate another country's intelligence agency. Work as if you are part of the agency. Gather important information and report back to HQ.

SLEEPER AGENT/OPERATIVE

Do nothing. Wait to be called on by HQ. Then follow instructions and complete your mission. Then wait again.

PROVOKER AGENT/OPERATIVE

Go undercover, pretending to be part of an illegal organization. (It's being watched by HQ.) Get the organization to do something to get in trouble with local police.

How did you answer – Would you like to live in another country? If you answered . . .

1, your post will be in another country.

2, you may go undercover in the US or abroad.

3, your assignment will be stateside.

UNDERCOVER AGENT/ OPERATIVE PROCEDURES

You must complete these steps after agent orientation:

Create a **cover** as soon as possible.

COVER — identity, profession, activities used by an undercover agent to hide her true identity and activities

LEGEND — spy's claimed background or life story, supported by documents and memorized details

Back up your cover with a detailed **legend**.

HANDLER — case officer who is responsible for directing agents in operations

Arrange a meeting with your **handler**.

PROJECT MISS SING
CASE NO. 518

TOP SECRET

TOP SECRET

YOUR SECRET AGENT PARTNER, MISS SING, HAS BEEN CAUGHT.

NO WORRIES — SHE'S A MASTER ESCAPE ARTIST.

BACKGROUND:

Before your partner was captured by enemy spies, she left you a detailed, coded message.

DELUXE
DECODER
RING

PBIRE OYBJA.
1. PUNATR ANZR.
2. TRG QVFTHVFR.
3. ZBIR.

DECIPHER THE MESSAGE BELOW.

_____.

1._____.

2._____.

3._____.

1. YOU CANNOT USE YOUR SECRET AGENT NAME ANYMORE.

ASSIGN YOURSELF A NEW NAME. LOOK FOR THE FIRST LETTER
OF YOUR FIRST NAME (BOLD BLACK TYPE) IN THIS LIST.

ARTEMIS	**H**ERA	**O**PHELIA	**V**IVIANNA
BRIGITTE	**I**ONA	**P**HOEBE	**W**ELLA
CALLISTA	**J**EWEL	**Q**UEEN	**X**ENA
DOVE	**K**ARA	**R**OXANNE	**Y**UNA
ELECTRA	**L**EXI	**S**ABINE	**Z**ELDA
FIONA	**M**AXINE	**T**ATIANA	
GISELLE	**N**ATASHA	**U**RSULA	

NOW LOOK FOR THE LAST LETTER OF YOUR LAST NAME IN THIS LIST.

ARROW	**H**ALO	**O**LIVER	**V**ENUS
BLADE	**I**CE	**P**OWERS	**W**AVE
COMET	**J**ET	**Q**UILL	**X**AVIER
DOMINO	**K**ING	**R**AYS	**Y**ANNI
EDGE	**L**OVE	**S**ANTANA	**Z**ENITH
FLARE	**M**ARVEL	**T**EAL	
GRACE	**N**OBLE	**U**LTRA	

ENTER YOUR NEW FIRST & LAST NAME BELOW.

PROJECT MISS SING
CASE NO. TOP SECRET

2. CHANGE YOUR HAIR OR FACE.

COUNT THE NUMBER OF LETTERS IN YOUR ORIGINAL FIRST, MIDDLE, AND LAST NAME.

IF THE NUMBER OF LETTERS IS ...

10 OR FEWER,
WEAR A SCARF
AND EYEGLASSES.

21 OR MORE,
WEAR A HAT AND
SUNGLASSES.

**CIRCLE
YOUR
DISGUISE**

11–20,
WEAR A WIG
AND MAKEUP.

3. CIRCLE SOME PROPS TO COMPLETE YOUR DISGUISE:

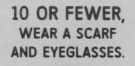

LIMO	HIGH HEELS
SEQUINED GOWN	DESIGNER BAG
CLUTCH PURSE	SPORTS CAR
TENNIS RACKET	TENNIS SKIRT
SURFBOARD	FLIP-FLOPS
TOTE BAG	GUITAR

4. RELOCATE TEMPORARILY.

USE THE MONTH YOU WERE BORN TO IDENTIFY
THE COUNTRY YOU WILL BE HIDING IN.

JAN	JAPAN	JUL	JORDAN
FEB	FIJI	AUG	AUSTRALIA
MAR	MONACO	SEP	SEYCHELLES
APR	AUSTRIA	OCT	OMAN
MAY	MOROCCO	NOV	NEW ZEALAND
JUN	JAMAICA	DEC	DENMARK

ENTER YOUR NEW LOCATION BELOW.

PROJECT MISS SING
CASE NO. TOP.SECRET

DOT CIPHER
PUT YOUR SECRET AGENT KNOW-HOW TO THE TEST

First top secret message from HQ

1. Carefully cut out this alphabet strip along the dotted line.

ABCDEFGHIJKLMNOPQRSTUVWXYZ

2. Place the alphabet strip on the first line of the notebook paper below.
Line up the left side of the strip with the notebook paper margin (red line).

3. Write the letter that appears directly above dot.

4. Move alphabet strip down to next line. Keep left side of the strip lined up with notebook paper margin! Write the letter that appears directly above dot.

5. Continue moving down notebook paper and writing letters. Letters reveal message from HQ.

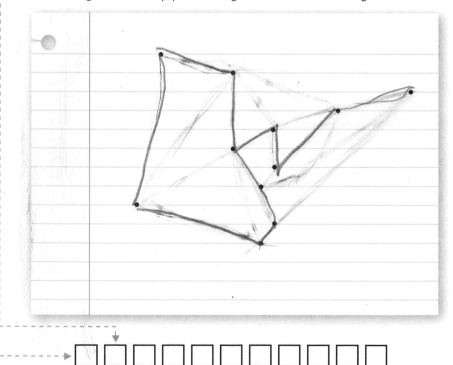

PROJECT HIDDEN JIM
CASE NO. 0756

CONFIDENTIAL

Legend has it that a rare diamond ring was hidden in this castle many years ago.

BACKGROUND:

THE CASTLE FAMILY HAS NEVER FOUND THE RING. LATELY, THEIR GROUNDSKEEPER, JAMES, HAS BEEN ACTING STRANGE. HE WALKS THE CASTLE HALLS LATE AT NIGHT AND HIDES WHEN HE'S SPOTTED. HE MIGHT KNOW SOMETHING.

Groundskeeper James

MATERIALS:

AN UNUSUAL SCROLL HAS BEEN PASSED DOWN THROUGH THE FAMILY FOR HUNDREDS OF YEARS. BUT THE WRITING ON IT DOESN'T MAKE SENSE. IT MIGHT BE A CLUE.

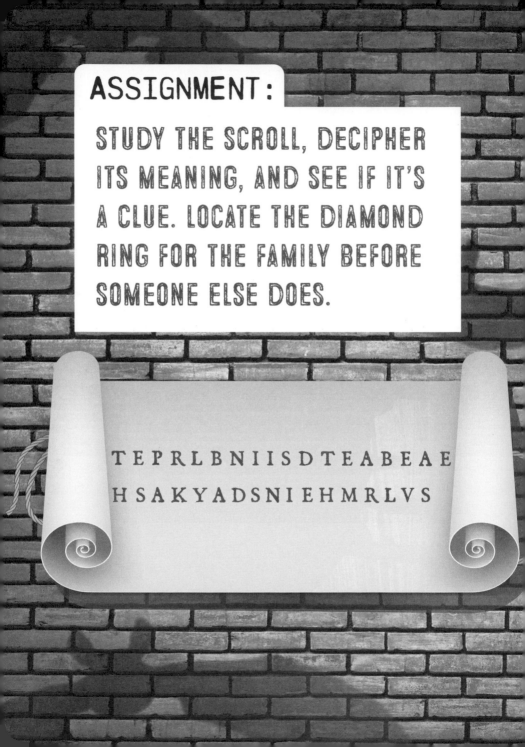

ASSIGNMENT:

STUDY THE SCROLL, DECIPHER ITS MEANING, AND SEE IF IT'S A CLUE. LOCATE THE DIAMOND RING FOR THE FAMILY BEFORE SOMEONE ELSE DOES.

TEPRLBNIISDTEABEAE
HSAKYADSNIEHMRLVS

T E P R L B N I I S D T E A B E A E

H S A K Y A D S N I E H M R L V S

LOOK FOR A PATTERN IN THE SCROLL. CONNECT LETTERS, MOVING UP AND DOWN, RIGHT TO LEFT, OR HORIZONTALLY LIKE THIS.

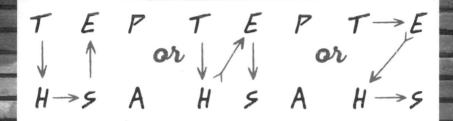

SEE IF WORDS START TO FORM. WHEN WORDS START TO FORM, CONTINUE CONNECTING LETTERS IN THAT SAME PATTERN. WRITE THE STRING OF LETTERS BELOW & LOOK FOR THE MESSAGE.

UNDERCOVER AGENT/ OPERATIVE PROCEDURES

You must complete these steps before reporting to your post:

COBBLER — (a.k.a. shoemaker) spy who creates/forges false passports, visas, diplomas and other documents

SHOE — false passport or visa

Visit a **cobbler** immediately so she can work on your **shoe.**

POCKET LITTER — items in an agent's pocket — receipts, tickets, scribbled-on scraps of paper, etc. that make her identity believable

Create some **pocket litter.** Stash it in your pockets, backpack, and bags.

PAROLES — passwords agents use to identify themselves to each other

Memorize your **paroles** and use when dealing with other agents.

PROJECT **MERM AID**
CASE NO. H2O

CONFIDENTIAL

FOR YOUR EYES ONLY

Treasure hunters have been looking for lost treasure off the coast of a remote island for weeks.

But they're about to give up the search.

BACKGROUND:

THE SUBMARINE CREW
HAS REPORTED MERMAID
SIGHTINGS DURING
THE SEARCH. MERMAIDS
SWIM UP TO THE SUB
AND TAP-TAP-TAP ON
THE WINDOWS.

PROJECT MERM AID
CASE NO. H_2O

DETAILS:

THERE'S A PATTERN TO THE MERMAID TAPS. IT'S A SET OF SHORT AND LONG TAPS.

ASSIGNMENT:

USE MORSE CODE TO TRY TO DECIPHER THE MERMAID TAPS AND HELP THE CREW.

MORSE CODE

A •-				
B -•••	G --•	L •-••	Q --•-	V •••-
C -•-•	H ••••	M --	R •-•	W •--
D -••	I ••	N -•	S •••	X -••-
E •	J •---	O ---	T -	Y -•--
F ••-•	K -•-	P •--•	U ••-	Z --••

CREW'S LOG OF MERMAID TAPS

DECODE CREW'S LOG TO FIGURE OUT WHAT THE MERMAIDS ARE COMMUNICATING.

PROJECT MERM AID
CASE NO. H_2O

Second top secret message from HQ

GN XRG ENVA GBC NE VF

1. Use your Deluxe Decoder Ring to decipher the letters. Enter the letters below.

SPACE CODE

2. Try changing the spacing between the decoded groups of letters. Words should start to form.

What is the message?_____

Third top secret message from HQ

QE VIRG BONEP RYB AN

Use your Deluxe Decoder Ring and Space Code to decipher it.

What is the message?_____

PROJECT PURR
CASE NO. 9

CONFIDENTIAL

FOR YOUR EYES ONLY

SUSPECT: CATHERINE B. ERGLER

AUTHORITIES BELIEVE WELL-KNOWN HEIRESS AND BUSY SOCIALITE, CAT B. ERGLER, IS STEALING PRECIOUS BELONGINGS FOR THE FUN OF IT.

BACKGROUND:

AUTHORITIES DO NOT HAVE ANY PROOF TO PRESS CHARGES. BUT THERE'S A RUMOR THAT SHE MIGHT BE HIDING STOLEN PROPERTY IN HER MANSION'S SECRET VAULT.

CONFIDENTIAL

PROJECT PURR
CASE NO. 9

LEADS:
HQ INTERCEPTED THREE NOTES FROM CAT'S PERSONAL ASSISTANTS. EACH NOTE IS A SET OF NUMBERS. HQ BELIEVES THE NUMBERS MIGHT BE CODES GRANTING ACCESS TO A SECRET VAULT.

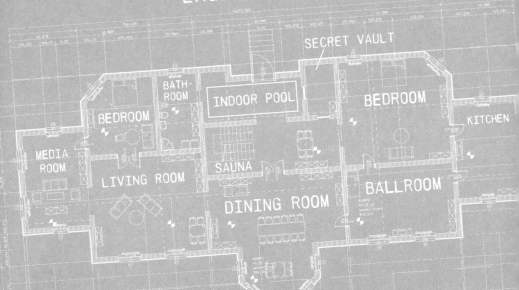

ERGLER ESTATE

SECRET VAULT

BATHROOM

INDOOR POOL

BEDROOM

BEDROOM

KITCHEN

MEDIA ROOM

LIVING ROOM

SAUNA

BALLROOM

DINING ROOM

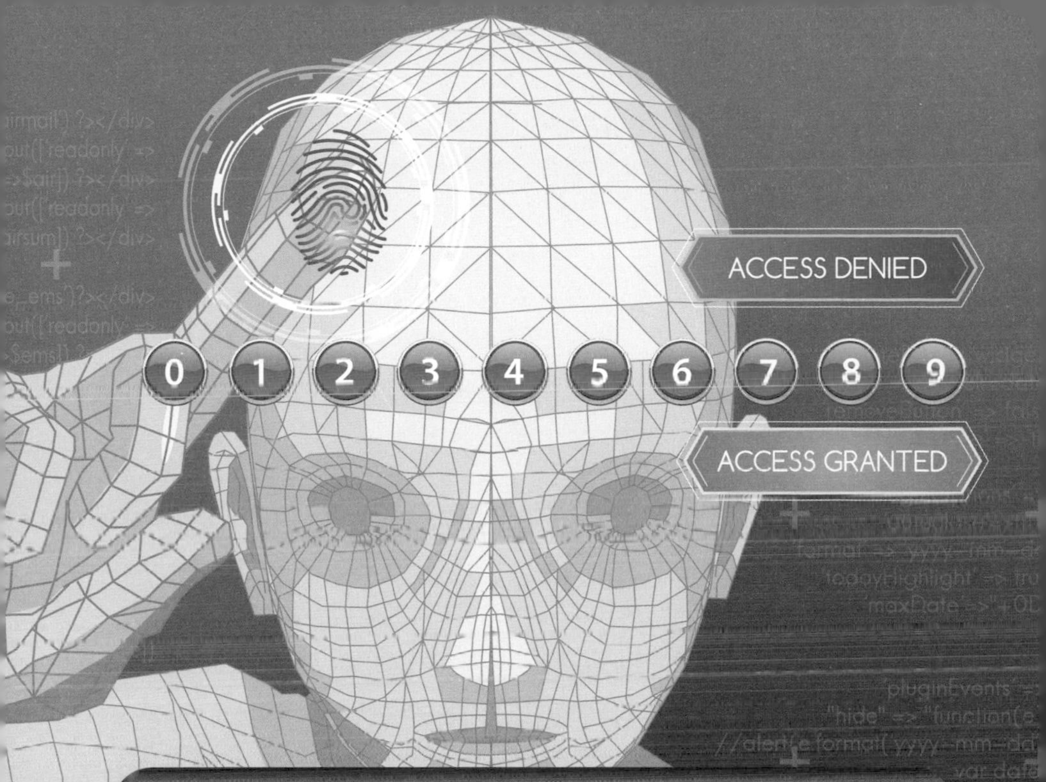

ACCESS DENIED

0 1 2 3 4 5 6 7 8 9

ACCESS GRANTED

ASSIGNMENT:

FIRST, DECIPHER EACH NOTE.
IF ONE OF THE CODED NOTES GIVES
ACCESS TO THE VAULT, DISGUISE
YOURSELF AS A GUEST AND ATTEND
CAT'S BLACK-TIE EVENT. LOCATE
THE VAULT, OPEN IT, AND TAKE
PICTURES OF ITS CONTENTS.
TURN PHOTOS INTO HQ.

PROJECT PURR
CASE NO. 9

MATERIALS:

USE THE GRID BELOW TO DECIPHER
THE NOTES TO THE RIGHT. EACH
LETTER = A PAIR OF NUMBERS.
U=45 (U IS IN ROW 4, COLUMN 5).
P=35 (P IS IN ROW 3, COLUMN 5).
SO THE WORD UP=4535.

THESE (2) LETTERS SHARE THE SAME NUMBER.
SEE WHICH LETTER MAKES THE MOST SENSE IN A WORD.

COLUMNS

	1	2	3	4	5
1	A	B	C	D	E
2	F	G	H	I/J	K
3	L	M	N	O	P
4	Q	R	S	T	U
5	V	W	X	Y	Z

ROWS

31 15 44 43 35 31 11 54
13 11 44 11 33 14 32 34 45 43 15

NOTE #1 DECIPHER

24 23 11 51 15 33 24 33 15 31 24 51 15 43
54 34 45 13 11 33 44 13 11 44 13 23 32 15

NOTE #2 DECIPHER

31 34 34 25 52 23 11 44 13 11 44
14 42 11 22 22 15 14 24 33 51 11 45 31 44
34 35 15 33

NOTE #3 DECIPHER

HQ

UNDERCOVER AGENT/ OPERATIVE MANEUVERS

Follow these directives for passing information:

BRIEF ENCOUNTER — any brief physical contact between a case officer and an agent under threat of surveillance

Plan **brief encounters** in crowded, public areas to disrupt any possible surveillance.

BRUSH PASS — brief encounter when an item is passed between case officer and agent. They appear to "brush" by or bump into each other

Complete a **brush pass** only if you believe it will go completely undetected.

LIVE LETTER DROP — agent follows a path on foot with document hidden in a pocket. Second agent, unknown to the first, "picks" her pocket and passes document to a **cut-out** or officer

Plan any **live letter drops** in advance.

CUT-OUT — person or mechanism used by agents to pass material or message safely

PROJECT **INSIDE EYES**
CASE NO. 22

CONFIDENTIAL

BACKGROUND:

AN ORGANIZATION OF ENEMY OPERATIVES

operative – secret agent

HOLDS MEETINGS IN DIFFERENT LOCATIONS FOUR TIMES A YEA

BUT HEADQUARTERS

CAN NEVER LOCATE THE

MEETINGS

IN TIME TO CATCH THEM.

PROJECT INSIDE EYES
CASE NO. 22

ASSIGNMENT:

GO UNDERCOVER AND INFILTRATE THE ORGANIZATION. YOU'LL BE A DOUBLE AGENT.

YOUR JOB IS TO REPORT THEIR PLANS TO HQ.

infiltrate – move into an organization secretly and cause its downfall.

double agent – a spy pretending to serve one organization while actually serving another.

intercept – take, seize, or halt.

EVIDENCE:

HQ INTERCEPTED A CODED TEXT MESSAGE FROM ONE OF THE OPERATIVES. IT MIGHT CONTAIN THE LOCATION AND TIME OF THEIR NEXT MEETING. HQ THINKS THEY USED A KEYBOARD CIPHER.

HOW THE KEYBOARD CIPHER WORKS

To code a message, find the letter you need to code on a keyboard. Then move either 1, 2, 3, or 4 keys **to the left**. This is your coded letter.

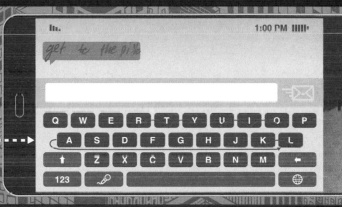

Try coding the message
YOU ARE A DOUBLE AGENT.

Base your code on moving 2 keys **to the left**.
Y=R, O=U, and U=T.

When you use a letter on the far left of the keyboard, like A, wrap around to the end of that letter's row for your first move.
Then move to the left. So A = K.

(Skip any punctuation or command keys on a computer keyboard. Do not count.)

YOU ARE A DOUBLE AGENT =
RUT KWQ K AUTCJQ KDQVE

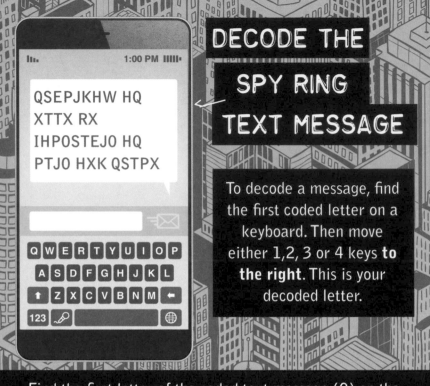

DECODE THE SPY RING TEXT MESSAGE

QSEPJKHW HQ
XTTX RX
IHPOSTEJO HQ
PTJO HXK QSTPX

To decode a message, find the first coded letter on a keyboard. Then move either 1, 2, 3 or 4 keys **to the right**. This is your decoded letter.

Find the first letter of the coded text message (Q) on the keyboard. Move either 1, 2, 3, or 4 keys **to the right**.

When you use a letter on the far right of the keyboard, like P, wrap around to the beginning of that letter's row for your first move.

Try this with the first coded word until a real word forms. Then continue to use that same pattern of key moves to decode the rest of the message. Write message below.

IVY AVE.

LILY AVE.

HWY 905

HWY 96

THORN AVE.

ROSE ST.

TULIP ST.

BOXWOOD RD

CROSSTOWN 10

HAWTHORN LN.

VIOLET ST.

4TH ST.

HWY 96

3RD ST.

HIBISCUS ST.

NULL CIPHER
PUT YOUR SECRET AGENT KNOW-HOW TO THE TEST

The note below contains a message within another message. The first letter of each word forms the original message (or, **plain text**) when strung together.

[**plain text** – original readable text; not a coded version.]

Fourth top secret message from HQ
Circle the first letter of each word within this strange message.

> Blue ostriches are really delightful. Fresh eggs regularly retain yolks. Take out trash after Nick gives Iona engagement ring.

What is the message? _____

Fifth top secret message from HQ

> Teach magpies French puns with powerful skills all July. Offer sticky buns and icy, frozen slushies. Coots can't offend ewes during Spring days.

Try circling the first, second, third, etc. letter of each word until you see words start to form. Once you do, write the letters down.

Write the string of letters below.

_____

What is the message?

_____

PROJECT SPY FLY
CASE NO. 004

CONFIDENTIAL

AN UNDERGROUND GROUP OF ENGIN

METAMO

HAS SUCCESSFULLY CREATED

THE FIRST-EVER

BUTTER

BUTTERSPIES RESEMBLE BEAUTIFUL GARDEN BUTTERFLIES. BUT THEY'RE REALLY MECHANICAL DRONES THAT SPY ON CITIZENS. THEY MUST BE STOPPED!

S FROM AROUND THE WORLD, A.K.A.

RPHOSIS,

SPY

STATUS:

YOUR SECRET AGENT PARTNER HAS DISCOVERED THE IDENTITIES OF THE ENGINEERS. SHE HAS SENT YOU A CODED MESSAGE LISTING ALL OF THEIR NAMES.

ASSIGNMENT:

USE YOUR DELUXE DECODER RING TO DECODE YOUR PARTNER'S MESSAGE. THEN TURN THE NAMES INTO HQ SO IT CAN LOCATE THE ENGINEERS AND CATCH THEM.

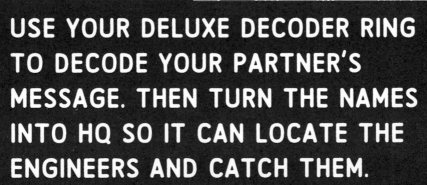

PARTNER'S CODED MESSAGE

ORN RRQYR
6 10 9 3

CNLGBA ZNAGVF
7 1 2 11

GNEN NAGHYN
4

ZBR FDHVGB
8 5

DECODE THE MESSAGE

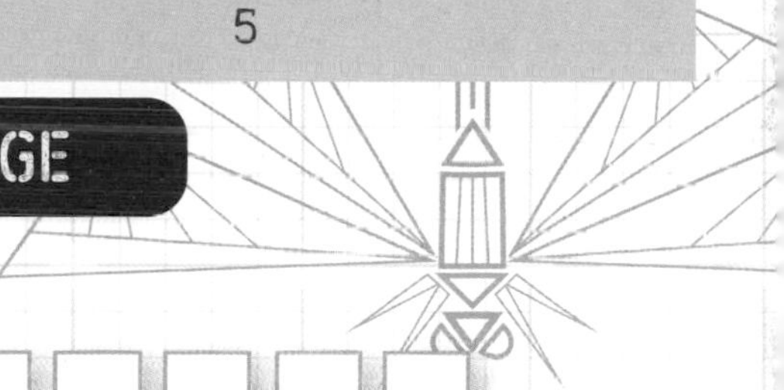

YOU STILL NEED THE NAME OF THE FIFTH ENGINEER. YOUR PARTNER MAY HAVE HIDDEN THE NAME IN HER CODED MESSAGE.

YOUR PARTNER'S CODED MESSAGE INCLUDES SOME LETTERS WITH NUMBERS UNDER THEM. ENTER THESE LETTERS IN THEIR MATCHING NUMBERED BOXES BELOW.

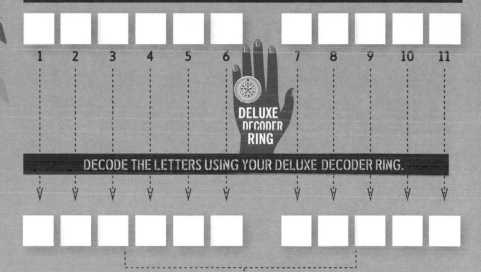

1 2 3 4 5 6 7 8 9 10 11

DECODE THE LETTERS USING YOUR DELUXE DECODER RING.

THIS IS THE NAME OF METAMORPHOSIS' RING LEADER. BE VERY CAREFUL. DO NOT FORWARD NAME TO HQ. SEND AN IMAGE INSTEAD. CIRCLE THE IMAGE THAT LOOKS LIKE HOW THE NAME SOUNDS.

TOP SECRET

DOCUMENTS & INFORMATION CLASSIFICATIONS

You may be granted clearance to read materials or hear information with these different designations:

CLASSIFIED — designated as officially secret; only authorized people may have access to

Classified information is marked **CONFIDENTIAL**, **SECRET** and **TOP SECRET**

CONFIDENTIAL
unauthorized release could cause damage to national security

SECRET
security classification above confidential and below top secret

more restrictions than confidential

unauthorized release could cause serious damage to national security

TOP SECRET
of the highest secrecy; highly confidential

highest security classification; unauthorized release could cause exceptional damage to national security

more restrictions than secret

MISSION NO NAME

TOP SECRET

FOR YOUR EYES ONLY

YOU'RE BEING SENT ON A SPECIAL COVERT MISSION.

ANSWER SOME TOP SECRET QUESTIONS SO HQ CAN ASSIGN YOU A ROLE AND START TRAINING.

START HERE

FIRST, CIRCLE THE ANSWERS THAT SOUND MOST LIKE YOU.

WHICH PERSONALITY TYPE DESCRIBES YOU THE BEST?

1. Loves spending time with people and staying really busy
2. Enjoys sports, setting goals, and competition
3. Likes alone time, studying, and surfing the net

WHAT KIND OF OUTFIT DO YOU FEEL CONFIDENT IN?

1. Cool, trendy look
2. Sporty, athleisure wear
3. T-shirt and jeans

WHICH CLASS WOULD YOU SIGN UP FOR?

1. Dance
2. Kickboxing
3. Language

YOU HAVE AN AGENT EXAM THE NEXT DAY. YOU STUDY:

1. with a group of other agents
2. after you get in a good workout
3. for as long as you can stay awake

WHERE WOULD YOU RATHER BE?

1. Front and center, totally in charge
2. On the sidelines, second in command
3. Behind the scenes, watching everything

WHO ARE YOU AT THE PARTY?

1. Really social girl meeting new friends
2. The one hanging with her circle of close friends
3. Girl who checks out the party but doesn't stay too long

WHICH SCENARIO SOUNDS THE MOST FUN?

1. Large, black-tie gala
2. 5K run or group workout
3. Testing out the latest, greatest smart phone

WHAT WOULD YOU VOLUNTEER TO DO FOR A PARTY?

1. Host the event
2. Serve food & drinks
3. Set up chairs and tables

WHICH SITUATION WOULD YOU ENJOY THE MOST?

1. Big concert packed with people
2. Bonfire with a bunch of friends
3. At home watching YouTube videos

IF YOU HAD SOME FREE TIME, WHICH WOULD YOU MOST LIKELY DO?

1. Call up friends and do something fun
2. Play a sport I love or work out
3. Read a book I can't put down

KEEP GOING

NEXT, ADD UP ALL THE NUMBERS YOU CIRCLED. IF YOUR TOTAL IS:

10-16, YOUR CODE IS — ZNXR PBAGNPG

17-23, YOUR CODE IS — THNEQ

24-30, YOUR CODE IS — JNGPU

WRITE YOUR CODE HERE.

USE YOUR DELUXE DECODER RING TO DECIPHER YOUR CODE AND ENTER IT BELOW.

DELUXE
DECODER
RING

LOOK FOR YOUR DECIPHERED CODE IN THE LIST OF MISSION ROLES.

HQ WILL BE PREPARING YOU TO:

MAKE CONTACT. You will go completely undercover, wearing a disguise so you can safely meet with enemy operatives to gather information. HQ will brief and drill you on significant enemy information.

GUARD. You will pose as the disguised agent's personal assistant. Your job is to protect her during any meetings with enemy spies. HQ will train you in martial arts and self-defense.

WATCH. You will monitor any exchanges that occur between disguised agent and enemy operatives from a nearby van. HQ will instruct you on how to use surveillance and wiretapping equipment.

ROUTE CIPHER

Sixth top secret message from HQ

GT EF TR DO OM CA UG ME EN NT

1. Outline a 10 x 2 grid (10 columns across, 2 rows down) on the graph paper.

2. Enter the letters from the encrypted message into your grid – start in the **upper left corner** of your grid and work your way **down** each column like this.

3. Now reading across each row from left to right, write the string of letters below. What is the message?

Final top secret message from HQ

TCIO NOWT EDCY MHYL UTNF

1. Outline a 5 x 4 grid (5 columns across, 4 rows down) on the graph paper.

2. Enter the letters from the encrypted message into your grid – start in the **bottom right corner** and work your way **up** each column.

3. Now reading across each row from left to right, write the string of letters below. What is the message?

PROJECT SECRET SENDER
CASE NO. 2050

POST OFFICE
04.08.2050
POST OFFICE

CONFIDENTIAL

FOR YOUR EYES ONLY

MYSTERIOUS
DOCUMENTS HAVE BEEN
SHOWING UP
AT YOUR HOME.

PROJECT SECRET SENDER
CASE NO. 2050

BACKGROUND:

YOU HAVE RECEIVED FOUR CODED DOCUMENTS OVER THE PAST YEAR. THERE'S NO SIGNATURE, NO RETURN ADDRESS. THEY'RE NOT FROM HEADQUARTERS.

LAB RESULTS:

HQ'S TESTS ONLY SHOW YOUR DNA ON THE DOCUMENTS. THE LAB HAS ASKED YOU TO WEAR GLOVES TO OPEN MAIL FROM NOW ON.

ASSIGNMENT:

STUDY THE DOCUMENTS AND FIGURE OUT THE COMMUNI-CATION. THE FOURTH ONE MAY BE A CODE KEY.

ABC	DEF	GHI
JKL	MNO	PQR
STU	VWX	YZ

THIS MAY BE A CODE KEY FOR
THE REST OF THE DOCUMENTS.
LINES ARE USED TO SHOW THE PART
OF THE GRID THE LETTER IS IN.
A DOT SHOWS WHERE THE LETTER IS
LOCATED WITHIN THE GROUP OF
THREE LETTERS. SO,

A = .⌋   B = .⌋   AND C = .⌋

M = ⌊.⌋   AND Q = ⌊.⌋   ETC.

USE THE CODE KEY TO DECIPHER AS MUCH OF THE DOCUMENTS AS YOU CAN.

Code key

A B C	D E F	G H I
J K L	M N O	P Q R
S T U	V W X	Y Z

DECIPHER THE FIRST DOCUMENT BELOW ⬇ DO NOT INCLUDE THE RED LETTERS THAT ARE IN THE CODE.

DECIPHER THE SECOND DOCUMENT BELOW.

DECIPHER THE THIRD DOCUMENT BELOW.
DO NOT INCLUDE THE RED LETTERS
THAT ARE IN THE CODE.

PROJECT SECRET SENDER
CASE NO. 2050

DELUXE DECODER RING

1. USE YOUR DELUXE DECODER RING TO DECIPHER THE SIX RED LETTERS [V, N, Z, L, B, AND H] THAT ARE IN THE ORIGINAL CODED DOCUMENTS. ADD THEM TO YOUR DECIPHERED DOCUMENT MESSAGES TO COMPLETE WORDS.

2. NOW WRITE THESE SAME SIX DECIPHERED LETTERS BELOW, IN THE EXACT ORDER THEY APPEARED IN THE DOCUMENTS.

WHO IS THE MYSTERIOUS PERSON SENDING THESE DOCUMENTS?

CREATE YOUR OWN
CODE OR CIPHER
BELOW. USE WITH SECRET
AGENT AND BESTIES.

PASS OFF
PENCIL THIN N

Cut out
this note along the
dotted line.

**WRAP IT AROUND
A #2 PENCIL
IN A**

*SPIRALING
MOTION.*

USE A #2
PENCIL WITH
FLAT SIDES.

BEW

MOVE THE NOTE
AROUND PENCIL
UNTIL COMPLETE
WORDS APPEAR.

TAPE BOTH ENDS OF NOTE TO
PENCIL TO KEEP IT IN PLACE.

WRITE
MESSAGE HERE

OTES

TURN HERE FOR MORE →

CUT OUT THESE BLANK
NOTES ALONG THE
DOTTED LINES.

WRAP A NOTE AROUND A #2
PENCIL IN A SPIRALING MOTION.

TAPE BOTH ENDS OF
THE NOTE TO PENCIL TO KEEP
IT IN PLACE.

WRITE MESSAGE TO A BESTIE ON THE
FLAT SIDES OF A PENCIL LIKE THIS.

MEET ME AFTER
CLASS TODAY

REMOVE TAPE AND PASS NOTE
TO A BESTIE. TELL HER HOW TO
DECIPHER IT WITH A #2 PENCIL.

SEND CODED MESSAGES

→

TURN HERE
TO GET STARTED!

GIVE A DELUXE DECODER WHEEL TO A BESTIE.

(IT MATCHES YOUR RING EXACTLY.)

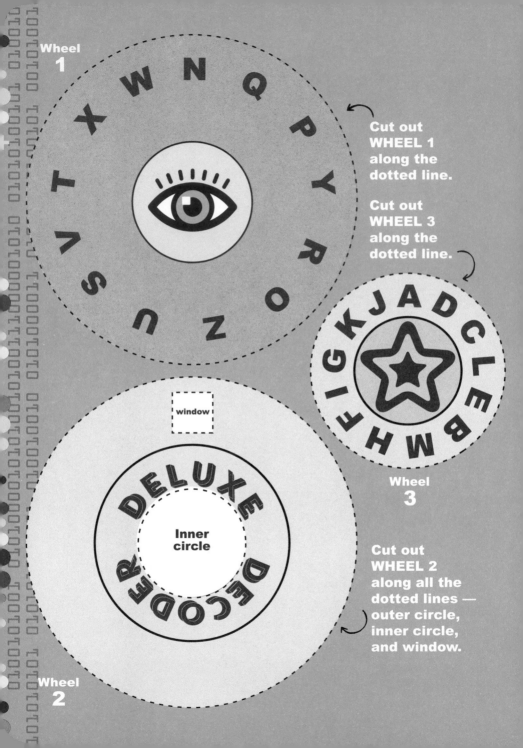

Wheel 1

X W N Q P Y R O N Z U S V T

Wheel 3

K J A D C L E B M H F I G

Cut out
WHEEL 1
along the
dotted line.

Cut out
WHEEL 3
along the
dotted line.

window

DELUXE DECODER

Inner
circle

Cut out
WHEEL 2
along all the
dotted lines —
outer circle,
inner circle,
and window.

Wheel 2

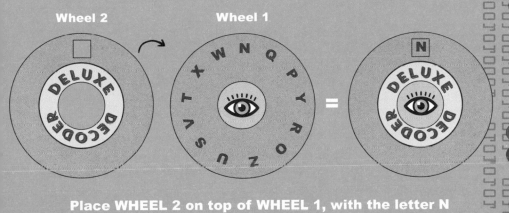

Place WHEEL 2 on top of WHEEL 1, with the letter N showing in the window.

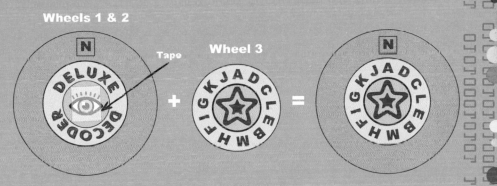

Keep Wheel 2 on top of WHEEL 1. Now attach WHEEL 3 to WHEEL 1 with double-sided tape or a piece of folded tape, with the letter A lining up directly under the letter N in the window.

Deluxe Decoder Wheel should look like this.

WHEEL 2 spins around WHEEL 3.

PSST, MAKE SURE N LINES UP WITH A.

SEND CODED MESSAGES

USE YOUR DELUXE DECODER RING
TO WRITE CODED MESSAGES TO YOUR BESTIE.
(MAKE SURE SHE HAS THE DELUXE
DECODER WHEEL!)

WRITE A MESSAGE ON A NOTE OR IN
THE MIDDLE OF A MINI ENVELOPE.
THEN CUT IT OUT, FOLD, AND TAPE SHUT.

PASS YOUR SECRET NOTE!

SOME NOTES
FOLD INTO
ENVELOPES.

ANSWERS

YOU ARE AN OFFICIAL UNDERCOVER AGENT
QBHOYR = DOUBLE
FYRRCRE = SLEEPER
CEBIBXRE = PROVOKER

PROJECT MISS SING/CASE NO. 543
COVER BLOWN
1. CHANGE NAME
2. GET DISGUISE
3. MOVE

DOT CIPHER
First top secret message from HQ – FLY TO LONDON

PROJECT HIDDEN JIM /CASE NO. 0756
THE SPARKLY BAND IS INSIDE THE MARBLE VASE

PROJECT MERM AID/CASE NO. H20
TREASURE CHEST IN UNDERWATER CAVE NEAR LIGHTHOUSE

SPACE CODE
Second top secret message from HQ –
TAKE TRAIN TO PARIS
Third top secret message from HQ –
DRIVE TO BARCELONA

PROJECT PURR/CASE NO. 9
NOTE #1 – LET'S PLAY CAT AND MOUSE
NOTE #2   I HAVE NINE LIVES YOU CAN'T CATCH ME
NOTE #3 – LOOK WHAT CAT DRAGGED IN VAULT OPEN

PROJECT INSIDE EYES/CASE NO. 22
THURSDAY AT
NOON IN
WAREHOUSE AT
ROSE AND THORN

NULL CIPHER
Fourth top secret message from HQ – BOARD FERRY TO TANGIER
Fifth top secret message from HQ – AGENT WILL FIND YOU ON FERRY

PROJECT SPY FLY/CASE NO. 004
BEA EEDLE
PAYTON MANTIS
TARA ANTULA
MOE SQUITO
5TH ENGINEER – MILLIE PEDES

MISSION NO NAME
ZNXR PBAGNPG = MAKE CONTACT
THNEQ = GUARD
JNGPU = WATCH

ROUTE CIPHER
Sixth top secret message from HQ – GET DOCUMENT FROM AGENT
Final top secret message from HQ – FLY TO NYC WITH DOCUMENT

PROJECT SECRET SENDER/CASE NO. 2050
First Document – THIS MESSAGE IS FROM THE FUTURE
Second Document – TIME TRAVEL IS REAL
Third Document – I KNOW EVERYTHING ABOUT   YOUR LIFE
Deciphered Letters – I AM YOU
WHO IS THE MYSTERIOUS PERSON SENDING THE LETTERS?
YOU